7 SEVEN
PRINCIPLES

*Creating Your SUCCESS in the
CONSTRUCTION INDUSTRY*

HENRY NUTT III

KP PUBLISHING COMPANY

ISBN: 979-8-9857184-0-9 (Paperback)
ISBN: 979-8-9857184-1-6 (eBook)
Library of Congress Control Number: 2022903064

Editor: Melanie James
Cover Design: Juan Roberts
Interior Design: Jennifer Houle
Literary Director: Sandra Slayton James

Published by:

KP Publishing Company
Publisher of Fiction, Nonfiction & Children's Books
Valencia, CA 91355
www.kp-pub.com
Printed in the United States of America

WHAT PEOPLE ARE SAYING

"*Seven Principles* serves as a roadmap for anyone in the construction industry who is searching for ways to create more value in their career. It also drives home the importance of maintaining a good quality of life, which too often gets overlooked. While the messages are vital, these principles are meaningful because they are expressed and explained through Henry's stories. Henry Nutt is a builder who has walked the walk and lived the journey. His trials and tribulations, shared with candor and honesty, will resonate with many builders."

—Keyan Zandy, CEO Skiles Group
and coauthor of *The Lean Builder*

"*Seven Principles* is a phenomenal resource guide that provides deep insights, life lessons, and steadfast drive needed to be successful within construction. It is such a powerful read where Mr. Nutt draws on decades of experience and shares many nuggets of wisdom, along with his inspirational career journey to help others in their overall career path. This book is essential to professionals at all levels to achieve goals, amount of experience, level of education, and no matter what career path."

—Dr. Giovanna Brasfield, CEO Brasfield & Associates

"The game has changed in our industry over the past few decades. Through sharing Henry's story, his book, *Seven Principles*, is a wonderful resource for ANYONE who is interested in developing themselves. Henry does a fantastic job outlining several principles that help equip the reader with the right mindset, soft skills, and determination needed to rise and thrive in the construction industry (or any other industry for that matter)."

—Joe Donarumo, VP-Field Operations Linbeck Group

DEDICATION

Rafael "Rafa" Palacios
1959–2019

Seven Principles is dedicated to "Rafa."
Because of him, communities are better, people can support
their families and a sense of pride and dignity was given back.

FOREWORD

1) Start somewhere = seed
2) Get a mentor
3) Refuse to be a victim
4) WORK HARD
5) Love what you do
6) Learn how to follow
7) Know the difference between
being a liability and an asset

A week before I was asked to write this forward, I was attempting to clean out my phone of old pictures and came across the image above. I was deleting pictures very fast until I came to this photo I took back on April 5, 2017. It made me pause for a long time and I thought, "can't delete this, I may need or can use it with my next class at CityBuild." Little did I know I would get a call from Henry asking to write the forward.

My first response to Henry's request was. "Are you sure you want me to write this? I'm not a writer," (in my interactions with

Henry over the years, one thing I learned about him is when he talks to you, he talks to you with confidence and not just in himself, you get the sense that he believes in you as well and true to form he expressed a confidence in me that I felt and couldn't say no.

A little about me, I'm a 55-year-old Latino male born and bred in Brooklyn NY. I myself am a product of community programs—once being a high school dropout , running the streets until eventually I did some of the things that Henry has outlined in this book. So it has been 30 plus years now that I have been working in various communities developing and running programs that help people become self-sufficient. I have spent the last 19 years doing workforce development in the Bay Area and the last 9 years working for the City & County of San Francisco managing the day-to-day operations of CityBuild Academy, a pre-apprenticeship program designed for San Francisco residents who want to get into the construction industry.

Henry has been coming to our program for years with his team from Southland Industries talking to our trainees about the field of construction and how to approach it to be successful and has hired a good number of our graduates who are very successful in the industry. The first time I heard him speak to the class I said to him "you should write a book" and he said I am.

What Henry outlines for trainees is very simple and straightforward, no games, no secret recipe, just straight truth, and advice for anyone who is looking to make a change in their life. Our trainees listen very intently when he has spoken and a great number of them have gone on to be successful in the field of construction.

In my opinion, this book is not just for people looking to be successful in construction, or contractors, union members, I believe it is good for anyone looking to make their way in any industry. I will definitely make this required reading in all my classes.

Chase Torres, Employment Liaison
Office of Economic & Workforce Development
City & County of San Francisco

CONTENTS

INTRODUCTION

WHY SEVEN PRINCIPLES?

It was approximately ten to twelve years ago while along with other members from Southland Industries, I began speaking to small groups of students at pre-apprenticeship programs in the Bay Area, with the first being the CityBuild program located in San Francisco, CA. When it is was my turn to speak, I found myself sharing my personal story repeatedly with a common theme of six to seven principles that seemed relatable, relevant, engaging, and even life-changing. Some came in the form of questions or everyday struggles that I could identify and share with my audience, no matter their background, current circumstances, or ethnicity. So-much-so that even the instructors began introducing my *Seven Principles* as I approached the platform to speak. They became a mantra they looked forward to hearing and one that I looked forward to sharing with each new student.

So, what is it all about? Will these seven principles change your world? I believe they can and will if you understand them and practice them with consistency and the appropriate mindset towards specific challenges you face regarding your career and aspirations.

As I travel around speaking at various non-profit organizations and educational facilities and working with larger organizations like AGC of America (Associated General Contractors) on diversity and inclusion in the workplace, I am sensing something new yet familiar with each audience. That something is the enormous momentum building around the country for a qualified, well-trained, and prepared workforce. A workforce that desperately needs to become a part of the existing dynamic teams that design and build extraordinary structures throughout the country. As the industry moves in this direction, it behooves each training facility, contractor, or association that acquires this workforce to recognize the importance of broadening the potential talent pool to people of various ethnicities, genders, sexual orientation, and religious backgrounds. The US Bureau of Labor Statistics reports that African Americans make up only 6% of the construction workforce. Women make up only 3% of the craft workers, so we indeed have a problem. The good news is the solution is intertwined within the actual problem, meaning we do not need to look very far to discover the answer. It becomes about recognizing the gap we need to fill lies within these demographics.

Unless we begin to take significant steps to access this untapped talent pool, the construction industry as a whole will continue to suffer through delayed project schedules and an exasperated workforce that simply will not be able to keep up. Ultimately, we lose as a country. So, we are indeed at a crossroads as an industry, and the movement to rectify the current situation needed to happen yesterday.

What is different today than approximately thirty years ago? One fact is the amount of work that exists versus the current workforce available to perform, has significantly declined. Several key factors contributing to this deficiency are minimal early exposure to the industry among youth, poor recruitment, a lack of vocational classes in schools, and parental skepticism about construction as a viable career option. Therefore, we must engage every resource available to create partnerships that bridge the gaps to training and ultimately hiring these folks today. "Workforce development will prove to be the greatest challenge to contractors around the world in the next ten years."—SMACNA Horizon 2013.

Even for myself, I wanted to quit at the beginning of my journey as a pre-apprentice. I asked myself, "Why did I get into this trade? I am not treated fairly. I am the first to be laid off, but I know that I am qualified." I often wondered if I was simply destined to be a guy that worked a few months out the year because I was not connected to the right groups, didn't know the right people, and, yes, often thought that I was the wrong skin color. Even with that, as blatant as it was at times, I refused to quit. As a boy, I was fortunate enough to watch my father go to work every day as a bartender, sheet metal worker, and eventually own his own sheet metal company. Because of the many great examples that he conveyed and taught me through his actions, I developed a work ethic that would prove essential for my ultimate success as a sheet metal worker. I cannot say I knew that back then, but I ultimately believe all things work together for good. I learned that you could not quit because it gets complicated.

Do not get me wrong; there were no freebies. On the contrary, progress required hard work and dedication. Still, I was thankful for a few men that I met along the way, in addition to my father. They gave me pep talks and encouragement at the appropriate times because I certainly felt like throwing in the towel on more than on a few occasions.

So here I am today, trying to provide the same advice given to me by my father and several other respected people while on my journey to becoming what I am today; a contractor with a mindset to be successful in whatever I chose to do. Additionally, it was essential to acquire a "quitting is not an option" mentality. Developing a "can do" mindset is such a critical aspect of learning the tools of the trade. Therefore, I wrote *Seven Principles* so it could become your own personal "pep talk" and hopefully answer questions while you are on your way to becoming the next leader (or whatever you desire to become) in the construction industry.

Although I understand that not much can replace hard work, what people need is an opportunity with tangible support and realistic goals devoid of biases. This potential employee needs the chance to prove that they have what it takes to help a company grow and become profitable, but all too often, it is an opportunity that rarely occurs. As a foundation of good mentors, family support, and lots of ambition, is vital, I know that going alone in this line of work is challenging due to stiff competition and limited positions available to potential applicants. I hope that this book will offer guidance and that the other community support systems rally around you to assist you in becoming the best that you can be for a company and ultimately gainfully employed.

I am not claiming that *Seven Principles* is the cure-all for the entire workforce crisis. Still, it will identify essential components for developing a workforce that is sustainable, stable, and worthy of hiring. I will continue to create partnerships with the committed agencies and organizations that work so tirelessly to provide the next generation of construction leaders across the country

Now when I say that my book is not the cure-all, I genuinely mean that. But, I am confident that I have a relevant story to share. I believe my story will be useful to others.

During my early years working with some of the pre-apprenticeship programs, I hired someone I believed to be a promising worker. For his protection, I will call him Marcus. Like us all, Marcus had a story. His background was, let me say, typical of someone growing up without many opportunities or a stable home. Even so, Marcus impressed me because he seemed to have a good heart and just needed someone to give him a chance. In addition, he was married with children and was committed to his family, which is always a good attribute when seeking a dedicated employee.

After some routine vetting, we decided to give Marcus the chance he wanted and deserved, in my opinion. He came to work, and everyone loved him. He showed up every day, on time, and with a pleasant attitude, which I might add are critical characteristics of a key employee. He had no complaints from anyone. He was slowly becoming the poster child for what a pre-apprenticeship agency should exemplify with their clientele.

After much hard work and studying, Marcus ultimately passed the state apprenticeship test and began to serve his apprenticeship with Southland Industries. He worked on a large project for several months when I received a call about some potential theft occurring on the project. Unfortunately, Marcus' name was involved, along with a couple of other employees. I was very disappointed by the news but equally determined to understand what occurred so that our team based any decisions we ultimately made on facts versus hearsay.

Once my general foreman and I conducted several interviews and received an unprovoked confession from one of the identified perpetrators, we concluded that the stories were true with hard-proven facts. As a last-ditch effort to allow the remaining culprits (including Marcus) to come clean, we sat them down to share what we knew about their scheme. At that time, none of them were willing to "rat" one another out, but we had facts and clearly expressed them. Unfortunately, they still stood firm with endless excuses and explanations, so we were forced to fire them all on the spot.

That was one of the worst days of my career as a general superintendent because Marcus became like family. He was my rising star and a tangible example of what it looks like when companies support these types of programs and the people in them. I reflected on the day when I brought Marcus to my office and told him I would give him an opportunity and hire him. I remember how grateful he was when he said, "Mr. Nutt, I will not let you down."

Now I understand that no one is perfect, and in this business, "shit happens." So, I chalked it up as a lesson learned (that hurt) for both sides and pressed on. After we all departed from that heated exchange, I decided to drive home versus going back to the office. To my amazement, I received an unexpected phone call from Marcus. He wanted to admit what he did with a heartfelt apology. I thanked him for his confession and accepted his apology. Unfortunately, it was not going to change the outcome of his termination, but it did allow me the opportunity to share some final words with Marcus and enable him to leave with a bit of dignity and peace of mind for me. The rest is history, and now almost ten years later, I have not spoken to him since.

That said, I still believe in partnering with programs that prepare men and women to enter the trades, and thankfully I have experienced more successes than I have endured failures. And like I preach to my teams, if you are not failing at times, it probably means you are not doing much. This particular failure strengthened our process by identifying a blind spot and appropriately correcting it.

So, as you are reading *Seven Principles,* pay close attention to which one or more principles you relate to the most. Usually, the one or two that seem to give you the sharpest sting is the one or two that you should recognize as a place to start. The journey towards your destiny as a productive, safe, and sought-after construction professional within the construction industry should begin with that in mind.

MY
JOURNEY

CHAPTER 1

I graduated from high school in 1986, intending to become a mechanical engineer. I was not sure what specific industry I wanted to pursue, but I assumed I would figure it out at some point. So off to a junior college I went, with plans to transfer to a four-year college within two years. I worked at a local department store and went to school full-time for about a year and a half when my father proposed that I take the test to become a sheet metal worker. I confess, it was the last thing on my mind and entirely far away from what my ultimate plans were, or so I thought. Like any young person, I had my dreams and was unsure if I wanted to follow my father's footsteps into the trades, but I was also wise for my years at nineteen and knew I had nothing to lose by simply taking the test.

I took the Sheet Metal Worker's entry exam at Laney College in Oakland, California, a step that would forever change the course of my career path and my life, respectively. It took a few weeks to obtain the results, but once I realized that I passed the test, I had to make some decisions quickly about my next steps. This included quitting junior college, quitting my current job at

Macy's, and changing the comfortable flow I had become accustomed to for about eighteen months.

Although I was not inclined to leave my current situation, I did recognize that this was an opportunity that I could not just walk away from. So, with some good advice from my father about what it could mean to become a sheet metal worker, I took the plunge and began working almost immediately.

I wish I could tell you it was all gravy, but it was far from it. On my first day on the job, the company's owner yells at me for using the wrong tool to perform a specific task in the shop. My foreman said to him, "Give him a break; it's his first day." The owner replied, "I don't care if it is his last day!" That was my rude awakening to the harshness of the sheet metal trade and to many more days of frustration and a belief that this trade was just not for me. In my next job, I worked on the now-established Santa Rita Prison in Santa Rita, California. I was utterly clueless and not grasping the business. While installing heavy gauge cages around duct runs, my foreman called my apprentice coordinator to inform him I was not making- the-cut with the installation I was responsible for , even though no one ever showed me how to install it properly as an inexperienced first-year apprentice. I was deeply frustrated and ready to quit after less than one year of becoming an apprentice, but then I ran into two individuals at different times that genuinely encouraged me not to give up.

Maybe they saw it on my face because I had never shared my true feelings with anyone about this.

Thankfully I took their advice and continued down the path to becoming a journeyman. I rotated every six months, structured by the (JATC) Joint Apprenticeship Training Committee, and was beginning to learn about the many facets of the trade. I found that my forte was working in the field because I enjoyed being outside and working at different locations. I was finally beginning to feel like things were coming together for me. So, as a third-year apprentice, I rotated to one of the larger shops in the Bay Area at that time and remained there until I became a journeyman.

For the next several years, I worked sporadically throughout the year averaging about six to eight months of employment with a few companies. I had become discouraged and once again felt I had made a mistake with my career choice. So, after getting laid off again from another company, I decided it was time to make some changes.

I was newly married and decided, with some advice from my (former) wife, it was time to quit the trade, get a temporary job and return to school to pursue a career in counseling. So I began working a temporary job helping students in a high school while taking college courses in the evening. Although it was steady work and I had a goal in mind, there was still something not settling with the decision, but I continued for that school term.

Now some of you may think I am crazy, and I do not know what religious beliefs you have, if any, but one day after work, while on my routine fifty-minute BART ride home, I heard a voice, which I believe was God trying to tell me something. That voice asked me this question, which was, "Why have you quit the trade after completing the apprenticeship training?" I received training for almost five years and was about to abandon it, but I suddenly realized at that moment it was not time to quit. I shared the experience with my wife, and she adamantly agreed that I should continue pursuing work in the sheet metal trade. This moment proved to be the next chapter of my future, not just as a sheet metal worker but as a construction professional.

I began seeking work throughout the Bay Area for several months to no avail, but I was committed and would not give up. I had people laughing at me as I walked off projects trying to find work. Finally, one morning while at home, I received a call from my union representative about a job. Not only did he give me three options of where I could work, but just the fact that he called me at home was a confirmation of my audible voice experience.

I selected a job with a bustling company, and off I went, dispatched to a large mechanical contractor restarting my career on a six-day work week, 12 hours a day with overtime. Most things were the same, but during my one-year absence, I learned something new that I believe was key to my success and longevity as a leading sheet metal worker. I had to believe in myself, remember to take the initiative, and share my ideas regarding my project team's approach to work, even when I felt intimidated. My intimidation primarily stemmed from being surrounded by older white males with decades of experience. I was not confident, I was always waiting for someone else to decide, and I never shared my ideas even if I felt they were better or minimally valid. That attitude proved to be the perfect recipe for a mediocre construction professional, but the new and improved Henry was here now. Ready and willing to take on whatever was coming my way. At that time, I had no idea what lay ahead, but who ever does?

On my first day, I was a bit rusty, but I got back into the swing of things very quickly, like riding a bike. Making a name for myself was the goal; working hard and staying true to my newfound ideas about being a better sheet metal worker was the way I would achieve it. I recall one of my first jobs, my foreman set me up with a task, but he was not fully ready to show me everything, so I waited outside for a minute and realized, "that was my moment." So instead of waiting for him to return with instructions on a reasonably obvious job, I took the initiative, made a few reasonable assumptions, and began tackling the work. Once he came back outside and saw me working, his only comments were, "Oh, I see I have a leader on my hands." For me, that was it, stepping out and taking a chance with confidence in my ability! Indeed the rest is history, at least with this company.

I worked for Michael, my general foreman, for more than seven years and was eventually promoted to foreman while cutting my teeth in new leadership roles, which proved to be the groundwork for what was still yet to come. After my tenure I was finally up with Mike, I moved to another job site with a new general foreman named Raul. He had run some of the most significant projects for the past 25 years up to that time. We were unfamiliar with one another, but I was more than ready for the challenge. He had me perform a reasonably small job, which seemed like a test. What he thought would take two days, I completed in one, alone. He was impressed and asked if I would consider staying with him to oversee two large new ground-up buildings. I will admit that I was a bit nervous, but I told him to give me a day to think about it, and I would give him an answer the next day. So, I went home, spoke to my (former) wife about it, and returned the next day ready to embrace this new opportunity.

I was the newest foreman of three on his crew. I worked hard every day and was committed to growing and learning even more. Fast-forward a few more years, I was the last foreman on his crew and oversaw all the miscellaneous projects he inherited. I became his "go-to" guy. Eventually, Raul was promoted to general superintendent, and I inherited his area. I was in charge of all sheet metal construction in South San Francisco and parts of the Bay Area for several years. I had multiple jobs going throughout these areas with a relatively large crew. It was fun and exciting times. Eventually, I was promoted to general foreman, which required complex duties including estimating projects, procuring material, managing labor, coordinating with other trades, and interfacing with our customers while simultaneously ensuring we remained profitable and safe.

Several years later, I received a call from a former friend and colleague about moving to another company. At that time, he wanted someone to run a large project, but honestly, I was not interested because it did not offer me anything new, except a new hat, a new shirt, and a different company vehicle. So I opted to pass, but about one year later, he called me again. This time I have to admit his new offer made me pause; I pulled over to the side of the road so that I could hear what he had to say. Ben had recently received a promotion and needed the right person to fill his newly vacated position as sheet metal superintendent. I will admit that I was excited about the possibility but questioned whether I was ready for something like this just yet. Finally, after several weeks of thinking, prayer, a talk with my father and former boss for advice, I decided to take the job.

Approximately thirteen years later, with several published articles, a host of speaking engagements across the country, and with more than 200 people on my former shop and field staff, I was the sheet metal general superintendent of one of the largest mechanical contractors, Southland Industries. And just when I thought I was at my final stop in my career journey, our division leader approached me with a new opportunity approximately two years ago. One that has stretched me more than ever and has required me to recall the many lessons I have learned over the decades regarding confidence, humility, and sharp focus. This new role placed me in the area of our office that I always jokingly referred to as "corporate corner." I suppose as the new business development manager / preconstruction executive, the joke is certainly on me. But, like every role, I take it very seriously and have placed goals to expand, learn and operate like the veterans I am surrounded by.

There is not a week that goes by where I do not recall my start and how I got where I am today. It is pretty humbling, but I believe it is also a part of my destiny. I just needed to embrace the idea, accept it was possible and make it work for me.

These seven principles are essential to achieve a goal, no matter your career path, level of education, or life experiences. In the following chapters, I will share these seven principles in the most relatable way. I hope that you will be able to identify with at least one of them and that they prove to assist you as you embark on your career path journey.

SMALL
BEGINNINGS

CHAPTER 2

"Do not despise these small beginnings."
—Zechariah 4:10 NLT

I have always remembered this scripture from the Bible. For me, it captures a principle that exceeds religion. When applied correctly, it can help anyone remain focused on a long-term goal, especially when things seem to be in dire straits or start to feel and look unachievable. The principle is simple actually; beginnings are usually small. They look and feel small, and at some point, look and feel insignificant. Nothing could be further from the truth. Starting something new can be difficult, and typically we begin at a place where we need to earn respect. Who we are and what we embody is a mystery to those around us, and only time will prove otherwise. That said, it can become easy to get discouraged and doubt if we have what it takes to be successful. Nothing seemingly ever moves fast enough; however, you must remember that a part of the test lies in your ability to withstand the temptation to quit early or take a shortcut that fails to give you the experiences essential to initiate the next stage.

As we begin any new journey, we usually pursue becoming something more, someone more significant, or someone altogether new. This is a good thing and ultimately drives us to become more than we are today; however, if we focus too much on how far we have to go to accomplish the goal, we can quickly become discouraged. Our current conditions have a strange way of reminding us that not only do we have a long way to go to arrive at our long-term goal, but it will also cause us to question if we can truly make it there.

The doubts that fill our brains, the people that do not believe in us or the person looking at us in the mirror can become your worst enemy. For me, this speaks to everyone starting something new. We must consider our beginnings as an inspiration to propelling us to our ultimate destination. We cannot allow what we have not yet achieved or obtained as a license to remain behind or stagnate. On the contrary, these circumstances must be what we choose to utilize as a pivot to our next best thing.

Consider the many circumstances that destroy new beginnings like poverty, drug abuse, crime, racial oppression, self-doubt, ignorance, illiteracy, broken families, lack of confidence, and opportunities, just to name a few. Each of these can give us a legitimate reason to quit, or worse, never to begin at all, however as the scripture states, "do not despise your small beginning," for we all have to start somewhere. So, start where you are today no matter what! Your circumstances will not always look like they do now. But, as you move forward, one day, you will look back and realize how far you have come. You will recognize that things are different and make good progress, and the effort is paying off.

Now you must not compare your beginnings to someone else's. They are not the same because you are not the same as anyone else. You are unique; you are special and obtain your own set of gifts, talents, and experiences. We each have our own life to live, and how we choose to press through adversity is totally up to us, but if what you have been doing has proven to be ineffective, do you not think it might be time to try something different?

Perhaps you can look back into your family history and observe that no one has ever graduated from high school, no one had an actual career path, or most of your family lived in poverty. The question is, does this have to be your story as well, or will you carve out a new road for your future? Although the beginning may look bleak and feel the same as what you have seen all of your life, your next steps do not have to be. On the contrary, your next steps can be what opens the door to a promising future and career. You just have to believe it does and not get so caught up in what the beginning looks like because we all have excuses for why we cannot achieve a goal, but today is your day to start something new. It is time that you begin to defy the odds of your past and envision a better future for yourself, your family, and your community.

Just remember, everyone has a story, and none of us began where we are now. We have to put in the work and not allow our goals to become distorted by others and our unwillingness to "go through" the necessary complex and often frustrating stages of becoming successful.

FIND A
MENTOR

(or Hang Out with People Who
are Smarter than You)

CHAPTER 3

"Every once in a while, we all could use a helping hand."
—Henry Nutt, III

If you are anything like many of the people I have the opportunity to speak with, your group of select friends has not always supported you or provided you with the best examples to follow. Perhaps you are in the category of being subject to poor influences most of your life. The sad thing is we do not truly realize this until we finally desire to make changes for the better. Then it becomes a bit more difficult to break these bad habits that you have developed over your lifetime, because not only are they in your face, but more importantly, you are finally able to see them for what they are, obstacles. It will be challenging, but they are possible to overcome.

One way to do this is to begin spending time with people that are smarter than you. If by chance, you have been the smartest one in your circle of friends but do not have much to show for it, I would say that is a problem. Would you agree? The idea is not meant to demean you or denounce your level of intelligence but cause you to consider other avenues that can potentially increase your awareness and experiences. I am a firm believer in a scripture from the Bible that states, "Iron sharpens iron." In other words, we need to surround ourselves with people that support us, challenge us and even know more than us because from time to time, we all need someone else to help get us to the next level. How can that honestly happen if we consistently see the same things and have the same experiences with the same people? The answer is; it will not occur.

A countermeasure to this is getting a mentor or coach. A mentor or coach is simply someone that can help give guidance, expose your brain to new ideas, and model behavior that promotes success. They are typically someone who has lived the life that you are trying to attain. If you cannot physically find a living example that fits this build in your community, then try visiting a library. People that have something to say worthy of listening to have typically put it in the form of a book. Take advantage of what they know by exposing yourself to their words and experiences. The key is to expose yourself to new ideas and opportunities that will challenge you and encourage your growth and development. Remember, it will require discipline on your part. Reading a book or visiting a library may have not always been your favorite pastime but consider it as an investment in yourself and towards your future.

Now it is undoubtedly easier to remain where you are, but the outcomes should be so predictable that you are tired of what comes next and fed up with poor choices, dead-end jobs, and lame excuses that get you nowhere.

What is critical for you to understand in this chapter is that we all need help at some point in our lives. Still, suppose we continue to take ill-advised steps on our career paths, educational endeavors, or personal lives. In that case, we will habitually find ourselves on the short end of the stick, wondering what the hell happened and where did all the time go. Do not allow yourself to be that man or woman who looks back decades later about what you should have done or could have done. My question for you is; are you not tired of the vicious cycle of starting over and over again with no feasible end-goal in mind? If you are, then get a mentor, coach, read relevant books and research relevant topics.

A mentor will challenge you and quite possibly make you feel uncomfortable but do not allow yourself to become intimated by the introduction of change. Change rarely feels comfortable at the beginning, but running away at the first sign of fear or discomfort will block your success If your choices have not amounted to career satisfaction, dare yourself to try a new path. Are you or your family not worth it? The steps towards your destiny are up to you. So, do it, start today by soliciting some outside support. You can even reach out to me.

STOP BEING
A VICTIM

CHAPTER 4

"To have an excuse is to possess a reason
why you cannot achieve something."
—Henry Nutt, III

Ask anyone about their past, and you will hear a story, some filled with joy and others with tremendous hardship. For those who have suffered enduring hardships (me included), it can become effortless to make excuses about why you cannot achieve. Pursue and commit to endeavors designed to improve yourself, your family, and your community.

I can identify with being a victim in the workplace. As a Black man, I am very familiar with racism and preferential treatment for others in the workplace. I can recall many people laughing in my face when I was seeking employment as a young journeyman. I remember seeing others pass me by for promotions with less knowledge, skills, and experience, but they knew someone. They had connections that I did not possess.

I once lived in the victim mentality mode. I was typically the youngest person on my crew, as well as a person of color. I felt intimidated by everyone else's years of experience and seeming ease of problem solving in our day-to-day tasks. I often took a back seat when it came to giving an opinion or addressing a work plan. I felt inadequate within myself. No one ever had to scorn me because I carried the burden on my own like a tool-belt. It was exhausting, debilitating, and prevented me from experiencing any kind of success. It is what ultimately made it easy for me to leave the trade. After all, since I spent more time thinking I would not be successful in this industry, why keep trying? That was my mentality. That was me being a victim of my own set of beliefs and circumstances.

Somewhere along my journey, I learned that I had to first believe in myself. Why would anyone else, if I could not? I realized that the baggage of being a victim could not co-exist with a successful mindset. One had to die. I chose success.

As I speak to potential new hires in the programs I work with, I hear many stories about why achievement may not be possible, but I dare those same individuals to think about why they can achieve.

So, you came from a broken home, you are an immigrant, a woman, new to the industry, still learning the English language, or never witnessed true success in your family or even in your community. Yet perhaps you are the one to start a new path and set the tone for those who are watching you. Maybe you are the one to create something new.

A victim mentality will always find an excuse for coming into work late, not showing up at all, or failing to take instructions from their boss. Likewise, there will always be a reason that seems justified in their minds to defy authority, quit, or simply not show up at all psychologically and prepared to work.

Like many other trade managers, I seek to employ people who show up on time, are eager to work, are open to becoming a part of a larger team, are willing to learn, and want to work hard every day. It seems like common sense, but I am here to tell you there is nothing common about it, unfortunately.

A person with a victim mentality cannot fit into the mainstream of a thriving workforce because he or she will always find an excuse when they fail to meet objectives, defer their responsibility, or fail to find solutions. This mentality quickly becomes tiresome to a field leader and unfair to the team he or she is working with; therefore, removal from the crew is typically the outcome.

If you have found yourself exhibiting the victim mentality, recognize that this mentality leads to disappointment for you and your employer, even if the circumstances are genuinely unfair. You will be the first to be removed from a team that is striving to become better. Those who carry themselves as victims are draining and need maintenance that minimizes their value to the team. So do not become that person. Stop making excuses for what you do not know or why you have not reached a goal. As long as you are alive, there is still time to get there.

Look into the mirror of your own life and say, "This new day begins with me!." The past is the past. It's a new day filled with opportunity, and it is about time that I begin to walk in it!

So, if this is an area you need help with, the first step to improving is realizing you have an issue. The next step is to seek help on how to rectify it. The fix may not occur overnight, but it starts in the right direction when you begin to address it head-on. The next step would be to start implementing practices based on the new information you discovered.

I do not intend to oversimplify any issues or struggles that anyone has in life or propose a one-stop-shop cure-all approach, however, if you want to make it in the construction business, you need to have your game face on every day. We are highly compensated and our employers need to see our appreciation for the opportunities they provide, by us bringing our "A-Game" every day. Anything less is unacceptable. So stop seeing yourself as a victim to anything or anyone and work on ways to empower yourself with what you need to overcome in every situation that you experience. Think of a challenge as your opportunity to shine.

WORK HARD AND ALWAYS DO YOUR BEST

CHAPTER 5

*"At the end of the day, nothing will ever replace hard work,
and you will never choose to do your best
if you are only working for a paycheck."*
—Henry Nutt, III

Working hard seems to be a lost art with many people these days. We look for praise for doing the simplest of things at times. This mindset will undoubtedly short circuit your career path in the construction industry and any other industry for that matter. If you want to be successful, coming to work must be about the work and only the work. The praise, accolades, and promotions will come in due time. When your focus becomes about accomplishing the task in the most efficient and safe manner, you are on track for success.

As a kid, my father always had me doing something that involved work. Whether I was doing chores inside the house, pulling weeds in the front yard, or watching him change the oil or brakes in the family car. I learned very early that working hard was not only necessary but essential to maintaining a good and balanced life. Every day I watched my father go to work; sometimes, he had more than one job. He woke up early every day and always showed up without excuse. I had no idea how observing this would become so critically important later in my life and its influence on my career. He was giving me an invaluable tool that would prove to be the keystone to my success, which is known as a "work ethic."

So, what is work ethic, you ask? Well, let's break it down.

According to Webster's dictionary, "work" is defined as—
Exertion of strength or faculties; physical or intellectual effort directed to an end; industrial activity; toil; employment; sometimes, specifically, physical labor.

According to Webster's dictionary, "ethic" is defined as—
the principles of right and wrong that are accepted by an individual or a social group or a system of principles governing morality and acceptable conduct.

I do not claim to be a psychologist or linguist. Still, when I combine the two definitions, I would define work ethic as *a set of principles that govern how one views what is acceptable or proper when it comes to being employed, conducting a task, or performing work for an employer.*

Again, seeing my father go to work every day did something to my psyche, so as I became older, staying in bed late on weekends or not participating in the family chores was not commonplace. Of course, every one of us loves to sleep in from time to time but practicing that was not the norm as I was growing up. This pattern became a part of my DNA, directly tied to my experiences as a boy.

Your work ethic will establish how you choose to engage and pursue your career. Whether it is in the trades, college, or any other line of business, think of it like this.

How far can you throw a rock? Imagine that rock you have thrown is your goal. Your work ethic will either help you reach the rock in a straight line (which is the shortest distance) or have you moving in circles due to endless distractions and obstacles. Without an excellent work ethic, we will spoil our reputation and fail to reach our goals.

Case in point. When I was a first-year apprentice, I went to school twice a week from 7:30-10:00 p.m. So that meant after working eight hours somewhere in the Bay Area, I had to travel to school, occupy myself for several hours because it was too far to drive home, and return in time. I usually got food and took a nap in my car until class started. Once class was over at 10:00 p.m., I typically arrived home around 10:45 p.m. I showered and went to bed, only to arise the following morning around 4:30 a.m. to get to work on time (usually with 30 minutes to spare).

I did this at some level for my entire apprenticeship; although my class times finally changed after the first year, it was still challenging. The point is, if my work ethic did not align with the expectations assigned for work and school, I would not have made it through successfully. Instead, I would have found excuses or reasons to justify why it was simply too hard, which would have resulted in my prematurely giving up like so many people I know have done.

Some students I ran across had been in their apprenticeships for more than seven years, yet, they were still technically only second or third-year apprentices according to the actual hours in their schooling. I do not know why this occurred, but I imagine the lack of work ethic in the classroom was a contributor. As a result, they struggled and failed the program instead of seeking the help they needed to succeed.

Your work ethic is critical for success, and if yours has a history of keeping you down, it is time to change it.

Once I began working, I never missed a day. It did not matter if I were sick or not. I just showed up every day, ready to put in my eight hours for my crew. Something in me felt I would be letting them down if I were not there on any particular day for any reason. I saw myself as part of a larger team, and it did not matter if I was sweeping a floor, sealing ductwork, or fetching material; someone counted on me to perform that task, and I could not let them down by missing any days. Showing up was the only option, as I learned from my father.

Nothing will ever replace hard work nor substitute for it, hard work can offset other proficiencies that you may lack. For instance, when I first got started in the trade, I had zero experience in sheet metal. I was one of the first to arrive at work and consistently one of the last to leave. I performed my task and tried to anticipate the next move of my journeyperson. I was able to make up for what I did not know by working extra hard. Sometimes, this came in the form of studying longer for my classes, asking for extra help from my instructors or journeypersons, and always giving 110% at work.

As I gained experience working with other journeypersons, I realized that if I always gave it my all, asked questions if I did not understand something, and said, "Yes sir, no sir" to the instructions given to me, I would be successful. I was not always the smartest apprentice on the job site, but my colleagues could not match my work ethic. I out-shined others by simply working hard, and not kowtowing, and guess what, it worked!

I learned that even the grouchiest journeyperson would be willing to pass on essential skills and tricks of the trade to someone who showed effort. I recall many times during my apprenticeship where I had different journeypersons take me under their wings and show me what they knew. One, in particular, would yell things like, "I need an older guy." Of course, since I was only 19 when I got into the trade, I was typically the youngest on my crew, I was perpetually teased for it, but I took it in stride and made the best of it.

Guys like Virgil (a seasoned professional journeyman) helped me understand the "do's and don'ts" of the business, and I was always taking mental notes. I watched how he interacted with his colleagues and the other trade partners, and I took note of which people were laid off first and why. Sometimes, he and others taught me things that I should not do as a worker, I often learned just by mere observation.

Another great thing happening behind the scenes as you are working hard is the reputation you are building with your crew. As you will learn very quickly, the construction industry is a relatively small community, and you will go as far as your reputation will take you. If your reputation is established as being a lazy and unreliable apprentice, guess what? It will be tough to change that reputation once you become a full-fledged journeyperson. Your reputation will follow you and either hinder or promote your career. Think about that on every job you perform.

As you enter the workforce, never compare yourself to anyone. Yes, there will always be competition, and someone is waiting and willing to take your job. Still, if you acquire the discipline of working diligently and eventually add the required tools and knowledge, your only competition will be with yourself. So, do not become your own worst enemy by choosing not to work earnestly or by making excuses about why you did not or cannot fulfill a task.

"Give it your best shot" is a term I often heard growing up in my household. Still, I do not take it for granted that most homes receive that instruction, so take the information I am sharing as an essential tool to become successful with your choices for your future.

LOVE WHAT YOU DO, OR AT LEAST LIKE IT WHOLE LOT

CHAPTER 6

"When you love what you do, you'll never work a day in your life."
—CONFUCIUS

I know so many people that simply live for the weekend. It is all about Friday night and the remainder of the week is a blur or just time and space that one must endure. What a sad life that is! Think about it. We will spend most of our lives working somewhere, that is unless you expect to receive a significant inheritance from family or win the lottery. Would it not be nice if you enjoyed how you were going to spend the majority of your life? I mean, it is only forty hours per week, fifty-two weeks per year, less a two-week vacation, for approximately twenty-five to thirty years. Who or what else will get that much time of your life? The answer is, no one, not even our spouses, children, or best friends. So, it behooves us to think long and hard regarding the afforded options to choose our career paths. Sadly, some have no choices due to life circumstances, but if you are in the boat of people that do have choices, make them count. You will only impact the rest of your life with your decision!

Over the last several years, as I have visited different organizations sharing *Seven principles.* I try to encourage the students and clients to consider the options that lie before them. I challenge them to think of the experiences they have lived and the passions they have developed over their lifetimes. It is no accident that we each have specific delights and that we possess a unique set of gifts and talents. It is nearly criminal if we never choose to exert these talents and gifts in our communities or spheres of influence.

I understand that certain life circumstances do not always afford us the option to choose where we will work initially; however, we all have to start somewhere. The key is where we ultimately arrive. So what if you start with digging ditches or directing traffic for eight hours a day. The question is if you desire more for yourself will you end where you began or use the opportunity to stretch your options to something more gratifying, and lucrative?

I have been in my career since October 1987. I certainly did not start out enjoying going to work every day; however, it was not because of my tasks. It was primarily due to some of the people I worked with, but once I was able to get past that and, in some cases, change my situations (or even change myself); work became more pleasant and fulfilling.

Doing work that we love has many benefits. Not only will you excel at what you do for a living, but others will take notice and be impressed by how you choose to engage in your daily tasks. The attitude you exude and even your vibration will become contagious, and the ones that influence your tenure will be taking note of you. No one wants to work with someone who has a demeanor covered with gray clouds and negativity. We have all heard the expression, "Check your attitude at the door," that is almost impossible to do when you hate your job. Sure, you can fake it for a while, but can you do it for twenty-five or thirty years? My guess is no.

Statistics reflect that more than fifty percent of people working today do not enjoy their jobs. It's no wonder that so many people are hostile during commuter traffic hours, have short tempers, and are simply not very pleasant people to hang out or work with. My advice is not to become that person.

If you are restarting your career, hopefully, you are here not only because you have bills to pay. The specific choices you are making regarding your work-life are about the passion you possess for the work itself and the enjoyment it brings you. For some, it may take several attempts at a few different positions to discover what that passion is for you.

Although my position can often become stressful and include working long hours, I genuinely enjoy what I do. I leave my office or job site with a sense of accomplishment more often than not.

This in itself is rewarding and is actually like adding fuel to my tank. There was undoubtedly a rough period I had to go through during the early phases, and I still make mistakes along the way, but I am getting better. Not by chance or coincidence, but because I desire to get better, so I am deliberate about my growth and development. That is what you do and what it looks like when you love your job, or at least like it a whole lot.

LEARN HOW TO FOLLOW SOMEONE FIRST

CHAPTER 7

*"Every great leader had to first learn
how to follow someone else first."*
—HENRY NUTT III

I recall my first few weeks at Southland Industries. I had the opportunity to attend a training called "Project Team." Certain employees came together to learn about the company's history, company core values, leadership development and to meet the executive leadership team. Employees experienced about four days of intense educational sessions and met other colleagues. I remember one specific class with one of our senior vice presidents (Victor Sanvido). He posed this question to the class, "What one thing do all leaders need?" I thought for one second, and said to myself, "I know the answer to this question." Now I know the decent thing to do is raise my hand, but I will admit I blurted out the word, "followers." Victor immediately agreed, and my self-confidence soared at that moment.

So, what is the big deal about someone following someone anyway? Well, think about how essential leadership is in life and the workplace. There is usually chaos when there is no leadership, and equally, when poor leadership exists, there are typically people being led astray, which will ultimately lead to confusion. Have you ever followed a poor leader knowingly or unknowingly? Most of us can recall the disorder it created, so the significance of leadership, good leadership to be specific, is essential to any group or organization.

One of the first places to start your journey of being a leader worthy of being followed is to follow another great leader. This person may not be prominent or famous, but if they tend to be a person of their word, have good intentions, and pursues a worthy cause, start with them. Of course, for many, the mere idea of doing this (following someone else) will violate everything you understand and stand for, but remember this is about making new decisions and going in a new direction with your career, so pride cannot be a part of the equation.

Believe it or not, many leaders in the trades are waiting and willing to teach you their skills, but they first must recognize something in you. Something worthy of their time and effort. Will you prove to be notable? Here are a few ways that you can achieve this:

1. **Learn the art of saying, "yes sir, no sir."**—This is not a mandate to kiss your boss's butt, but get used to taking and

receiving direction from people that have authority over you without adding extra commentary. If you can get comfortable with submitting control, holding your tongue (at times), and take the direction, you will surpass many others in this business that struggle just with this.

2.   Always show up on time and be ready to go to work and learn.—The simple task of showing up before starting time with an attitude that declares, "I am ready to work and learn" is essential for success in this business. So, to be even more specific, if starting time is 7:00 a.m., you should arrive on site at least twenty minutes early. This will give you time to prepare for the day at a comfortable pace, and I guarantee your boss will also take note of your timeliness. On the opposite end of the spectrum, think about that person rushing to the job site late and unprepared. We all have an opinion of him or her. Do not be that person.

3.   Give your foreperson a reason to invest in you.—As I mentioned earlier, many current leaders are willing and able to invest in others, but the last thing we want to do is waste our time on someone that proves to be unworthy of our time and effort. And a little secret, we can identify this person within the first five minutes of working with you, so do not blow it or think you can disguise your genuine self. We will see the real you.

4. **Work to get the job done, not to earn a paycheck.**—
Many employees forget that the purpose of work is to get a job
done first that you will eventually be compensated for after.
Somewhere along the way, the mentality has shifted in the current
workforce. There is often an expectation of privilege with the
position without a proper understanding of the responsibility to
it. The "living for the weekend" mentality must die when you
begin to strive to obtain a carer, but keep repeating the same
actions if you just want a job.

If you can add a mentality of "work first," and be a team
player and follow sensible and safe directions, you will set yourself
up for success on your career journey.

BECOME AN ASSET VERSUS A LIABILITY

CHAPTER 8

"Live as if you understand your worth and your value, and others will begin to as well."

—Henry Nutt III

The difference between being an asset on a team versus being a liability is you will find yourself employed more often than not, while the others will wonder why he or she is consistently unemployed.

The sooner you can fully understand what value you bring to a team, the sooner you can become a part of that team for the long term. As I mentioned in earlier chapters, rarely will you be asked to perform past your expected ability or knowledge. We just want you to show up (on time), work hard, do as you are instructed, and be willing to learn something new.

The best way to grasp this point is to look at any team sport. For example; in football, each player has a role, from the quarterback to the person ensuring the players remain hydrated. When one of the members fails to perform their specific responsibility, the entire team will suffer. If you can begin to acknowledge the particular task you have as an employee, whether seemingly menial or significant, the sooner your employer, manager, or foreperson will see you as an asset to the crew.

When you contribute to your team, the part you are supposed to contribute, everyone will notice and begin to view you as an essential player. They will recommend you to others, and your reputation will start to grow. That is what happened to me.

I worked hard every day. Some days my job seemed uneventful, and other days it was challenging, but every day I showed up and gave it 110%. As a result, everyone knew that they could not only count on me to show up on time with a great attitude, but they could count on me to do my job with excellence, diligence, and safety.

The better you know your job, its primary functions, and purpose, the faster you will get better at it and be acknowledged for it. This is the type of mindset that gets noticed, recognized and promoted. It does not require butt-kissing or violating rules, just hard work. It is not rocket science. You simply need to commit to the effort and never give up.

WHERE DO YOU GO FROM HERE?

CHAPTER 9

What are the next steps after reading a short book like this, and how do you apply the lessons, stories, and wisdom to make it all come together? Well, first I hope that you understand there are no magic formulas, fast methods, or quick fixes. Nothing can take the place of hard work, dedication, and commitment to a worthy cause. In this case, the cause is your career, and you must first believe that it is worthy of all your effort. How much is it worth to you?

For me, it meant everything, and I would not change one aspect of my journey. The steps taught me lessons, especially the hard ones, and even though many of them bordered on the line of ill-treatment, I learned how to survive in this business and how to overcome even when things were not going well.

Once you understand what you are pursuing, you must remove doubt and the notion of quitting from your vocabulary. The work will be the work if that makes sense. And no, it will not be easy.

So, if you take nothing else from this book, take this; you are and always will be a critical component to a prominent workforce.

Even as technology changes, however we perform our daily tasks, it still requires you and me to work with others. Work requires our hands and minds to solve problems creatively, thoughtful insight to remove roadblocks, collaboration to increase synergy, and the skill sets to perform at a high level. If you must reinvent yourself or get retrained for a new type of role, focus on remaining on top of your game. Take advantage of essential training and adhere to the seven principles mentioned in this book. By doing so, you will place yourself in a position to maintain longevity in an often cyclical, highly biased, and sometimes unfair business.

Discover what trade or career path you are interested in and obtain all the information you can about it. Talk to friends, relatives, neighbors, or go to the local library until you understand enough to make an informed decision. Once there, there is nothing left to do but to do it. Pursue the mission with all your strength and will until you achieve your goal.

It will not be easy to accomplish, nor will it occur overnight, but nothing truly worth it ever happens quickly, right? So commit to yourself, commit to the mission and commit to the steps required to get there, and you will.

Where you go from here is a destiny with your name on it. A career that will not only allow you to provide for your family but allow you to identify, develop and utilize a skill that you may have not even realized existed. Continue to perfect it and watch doors open. Never settle and become complacent with small successes.

They are great, so celebrate them, but keep pushing towards the higher calling for your life. Look to achieve more than your mind can comprehend by humbling yourself and connecting with smart people that put wind in your sails, either directly or through a great book, as mentioned in Chapter 3.

The rest is up to you. Now go and get it!

SEVEN
HELPFUL QUOTES

1. Start where you are; "
   The journey of 1,000 miles starts with a single step."

   —Lao Tzu

2. Get a mentor;
   "Tell me and I'll forget. Show me and I may remember, involve me and I learn."

   —Benjamin Franklin

3. Refuse to be a victim;
   "Sometimes when you're in a dark place, you think you've been buried; but actually you've been planted."

   —Christine Caine

4. Work hard;

   "If you want something you never had, you have to do something you've never done."

   —Thomas Jefferson

5. Love what you do;

   "If you think that peace and happiness are somewhere else and you run after them, you will never arrive."

   —Thich Nhat Hanh

6. Learn how to follow;

   "Listen and silent are spelled with the same letters."

   —Author Unknown

7. Know the difference between being a liability and an asset;

   "You are the sky, everything else is the weather."

   —Pema Chodron

ACKNOWLEDGMENTS

Writing this book has taken many years, and my career has taken many turns since the start. However, none of it could have been possible without the encouragement, belief in my ability, opportunities, and motivation from several key people throughout the different stages of my life and career.

First, to my father, I would have never pursued the trades without you, but more importantly, teaching me how to be responsible and provide examples of what it looks like in real life. I will be forever grateful.

To my wonderful mother. Thank you for always believing in me and encouraging me along the way. Your words and belief in me will always feel like home. I love you dearly.

Mike O' Riley, the first field leader that gave me a shot. I am not sure what you saw in me so many years ago, but you gave me a chance, and it was with you that my job became a career. Thank you from the bottom of my heart. Your trust in me and jokes always made work fun. I hope you continue to enjoy retirement.

To the late Raul Guerrero, may you rest in peace. You were a friend and also gave me an opportunity that ultimately shaped my career. It was under your tutelage that I developed the skillsets of a General Foreman. I will be forever grateful for the opportunity you gave me that was so prolific and key to my development.

To the late Johnnie Gooch, may you rest in peace. Although I never had the opportunity to work for you or with you, I saw you. You were the first black man I saw in a leadership capacity and well respected by his peers in the trades. That made such a significant impression on me and allowed me to have the confidence that it could happen for me as well. Thank you.

Ben Rivera, it was you who hounded me for almost two years to come to Southland Industries. I recognize that you had to believe in me and stand behind that belief and often go to bat for me, even when I was unaware. I thank you for your confidence in me and the friendship that remains to this day.

Victor Sanvido, my mentor and coach, I appreciate you always having my back and demonstrating authentic leadership.

ABOUT THE AUTHOR

Henry Nutt wrote *Seven Principles: Creating Your Success in the Construction Industry* to provide the basic steps to help anyone successfully navigate the entry-level or pre-apprenticeship programs within the various vocational trades and explain how to remain successful for years to come. He has personally undergone the steps and fully identifies with many of the struggles, hardships, and obstacles faced while at this stage of a career journey within the construction industry. And although he does not claim to know it all, what he does know will help shed a ray of light on what steps to take (or not) to make it in this business.

Henry has worked in the Sheet Metal Union (Local 104) since October 1987. He has worked his way from a pre-apprentice to a sheet metal general superintendent and now to a preconstruction executive. Currently working for Southland Industries since May 2007, he has managed more than 200 employees on various projects in the Greater Bay Area in Northern California.

Managing approximately $1.5 billion in construction projects during his tenure as general superintendent. Henry is a strong advocate for diversity, equity, and inclusion by creating opportunities for a wide array of people. He works alongside several organizations to support initiatives and programs that educate and help others successfully navigate employment in the construction industry. In this regard, he has worked with organizations and programs such as The Associated General Contractor of America (AGC), CityBuild of San Francisco, America Works, BUILD, More Than Magic, and My Brother's Keeper Initiative with the Mayor's Office of San Francisco.

Henry is the current Chair for the Associated General Contractors of America Diversity & Inclusion National Steering Committee. The committee's primary function enables AGC members to connect and keep pace with the latest construction diversity and inclusion developments and create and drive associated initiatives. He and his family reside in Northern California.